Allie Learns About Alzheimer's Disease

A Family Story about Love, Patience, and Acceptance

by Kim Gosselin

Written for the Special Family and Friends™ series

JayJo Books, L.L.C.

Publishing Special Books for Special Kids®

Allie Learns about Alzheimer's Disease
© 2001 Kim Gosselin
Edited by Karen Schader

No part of this book may be reproduced or transmitted in any form or by any means, electronic or mechanical, including photocopying, recording, or by any information storage and retrieval system without written permission from the publisher. All rights reserved. Printed in the United States of America.

Published by
JayJo Books, LLC
A Guidance Channel Company
Publishing Special Books for Special Kids®

JayJo Books is a publisher of books to help teachers, parents, and children cope with chronic illnesses, special needs, and health education in classroom, family, and social settings.

Library of Congress Control Number: 2001087644
ISBN 1-891383-15-9
First Edition
First book in our *Special Family and Friends*™ series

For information about
Premium and Special Sales, contact:
JayJo Books Special Sales Office
P.O. Box 213
Valley Park, MO 63088-0213
636-861-1331
jayjobooks@aol.com
www.jayjo.com

For all other information, contact:
JayJo Books
A Guidance Channel Company
135 Dupont Street, P.O. Box 760
Plainview, NY 11803-0760
1-800-999-6884
jayjobooks@guidancechannel.com
www.jayjo.com

Dedication

This book is dedicated in memory of my own grandmother, who also lived with Alzheimer's disease. I shall treasure my special time and traditions with her forever and always.

About the Author

Recognizing the need for books to help children understand adult medical conditions, Kim Gosselin created the Special Family and Friends™ series. She is the author of the first book in the series, Allie Learns about Alzheimer's Disease, which draws on her own experience when her grandmother was diagnosed with Alzheimer's disease.

Kim is the author of 12 children's health education books. She began her writing career with a heartfelt desire and determination to educate the classmates of children with special needs and/or chronic conditions. Kim created the Special Kids in School® series, which covers topics such as diabetes, asthma and allergies, seizure disorders, attention deficit disorder, cerebral palsy, cancer, and cystic fibrosis. She also created the Substance Free Kids® series and the Healthy Habits for Kids™ series.

Kim now resides and writes in Missouri. She is extremely committed to bringing the young reader quality health education, while raising important funds for medical research. She is an avid supporter of the American Lung Association, American Cancer Society, the Epilepsy Foundation of America, American Diabetes Association, Juvenile Diabetes Research Foundation, and CHADD. For her work with children with chronic diseases, Kim received the National American Lung Association Presidential Award. Kim is also a member of the Authors Guild, the Publishers Marketing Association, and the Society of Children's Book Writers and Illustrators.

Allie tied the laces of her polka-dot sneakers. "I'll be down in a few minutes," she shouted to her mother.

Today was Allie and Grandma's Saturday morning tradition! Once a month, Grandma took Allie out for an all-day shopping trip. During the day, they always stopped for a fancy lunch with real cloth napkins and teacakes for dessert.

Allie could hardly contain herself as she snapped a white barrette into her long, dark hair. Allie loved spending time with Grandma. She always had fun stories to tell Allie about the "old days." Allie learned all about when Grandma's family came to the United States. Grandma was only a little baby when her family sailed across the wide blue ocean from Sweden. At the time, Grandma wasn't much older than Allie's little brother, Matthew!

"Coming, Mom," she yelled, sliding down the wooden banister.

Little Matthew played with plastic pots and pans while Allie and her mother waited for Grandma to arrive. She was nearly fifteen minutes late. Grandma was never late. She liked to come over early, so she had enough time to scoop up Matthew and make him giggle. Grandma was so much fun!

Allie's mom began to worry as she glanced at the kitchen clock. Several times during the last few months Allie's mother had noticed changes in Grandma's behavior. She was starting to be forgetful and even got lost in the grocery store once!

Mrs. Stevens dialed Grandma's telephone number. There wasn't any answer. Maybe Grandma was on her way. Together, Allie and her mother waited another fifteen minutes. Mrs. Stevens telephoned Grandma one more time. After getting no answer again, she decided to go check on her in person.

Allie helped buckle Matthew in his car seat for the short trip to Grandma's house. As soon as the house came into view, Allie and her mother could see Grandma pacing back and forth in the middle of her driveway. After they parked the car at the curb, they could hear her talking to herself and wringing her hands. Her purple pocketbook lay on the grass beside her, its contents strewn about.

"Grandma, what's wrong?" Allie's mother asked with great concern.

"That BOY!" Grandma said angrily. "He took my keys again!"

Allie's mother reached in her own purse and quickly pulled out Grandma's extra house key. Allie carried her little brother into the house as her mother gently led Grandma inside.

Grandma wasn't acting like herself at all! Allie was worried. She even felt a little afraid of Grandma's strange behavior. Mrs. Stevens settled Grandma into her favorite old rocking chair. She gathered a few wooden blocks for Matthew to play with from Grandma's special drawer, and sat him on a quilt on the floor. Asking Allie to stay with them, she hurriedly went into the kitchen to brew some herbal tea. It was Grandma's favorite!

"That neighbor boy must have done it!" insisted Grandma, sipping tea from one of her best blue china cups. "He collected for the newspaper this morning, and I let him inside for a cookie and a glass of milk."

Allie's mother didn't know what to say. She doubted Grandma's story, since she had known the paperboy and his family almost her whole life. They still lived right next door to Grandma. Often, the family helped Grandma with errands or snow shoveling during the winter.

Allie dipped her spoon into Grandma's flowered sugar bowl. Clank went the spoon! Allie peered down into the bowl. Her round brown eyes grew as big as saucers! There, resting on top of the sugar, was Grandma's set of keys!! Allie scooped them out with her teaspoon, shook the sugar off, and handed them to Grandma.

Grandma's face was pink with embarrassment. "Now, how did this happen?" she asked, confused. "That boy must have played a trick on me," she insisted. "Why, he sat right here at this table when he ate his cookie!"

Like her mother, Allie didn't believe the paperboy would have hidden Grandma's keys. He was nice ... for a boy! Whatever was going on with Grandma, Allie didn't like it!

Allie's mother was baffled. Grandma was getting older now, she thought to herself. She had been forgetting things lately too. But Grandma's behavior today seemed much more serious. Mrs. Stevens made a mental note to take Grandma in for a checkup with her doctor as soon as possible.

Clearing the table, Mrs. Stevens decided she had better postpone Grandma and Allie's shopping trip. Allie's mother took her aside and explained that Grandma probably wasn't feeling up to shopping that day. Allie was disappointed. She didn't understand what was happening. Nobody did.

Later that evening, Allie's mom and dad talked quietly in the den. Allie could hear soft voices coming through the big wooden door.

Mr. Stevens was as worried as Mrs. Stevens when he learned what happened with Grandma earlier that day. He too had noticed some disturbing changes in her behavior. Only a few days earlier, he had stopped by Grandma's house. He found her gas stove on. A sticky pot had been removed long before and sat in the sink. Grandma had forgotten to turn her stove off!

The following week Mrs. Stevens took Grandma for a checkup. Allie's grandma had lots of tests done by different doctors and nurses at the hospital's clinic. They took blood from Grandma's arm, took her in for x-rays, and did many other tests. The doctors talked to Grandma for a long time. Near the end of the afternoon, they asked to speak to Mrs. Stevens alone.

The doctors and nurses thought that Allie's grandma had a condition called Alzheimer's disease. Although it was often hard for doctors to diagnose, most of them agreed that Allie's grandma had many of the usual symptoms: memory loss, mood changes, personality changes, and poor judgment, among others.

The doctors explained to Mrs. Stevens that people living with Alzheimer's disease were different from each other. Some patients had just a few symptoms; some had a lot. Often, it took a long time before people were correctly diagnosed. Sometimes when people living with Alzheimer's started showing symptoms, others thought they were just getting older or becoming "senile."

Mrs. Stevens' heart sank. Still, she felt happy that Grandma was physically healthy. She was told there were many different medicines and treatments that might help Grandma. Someday, there might even be a cure. She knew it was important to think about the positive things. That's exactly what she would tell Allie!

Shortly after supper, Allie and her parents had a family meeting. Matthew was too little to understand what was happening. Allie held him close. Allie's mom explained everything the doctors had told her about Grandma's condition, Alzheimer's disease.

Allie was confused. She didn't understand. She wanted everything to stay the way it was before Grandma had Alzheimer's disease. Allie felt sad. Her tears splashed on little Matthew's head. Then her mother said something that suddenly brought a big grin to Allie's face. Allie's parents had decided to bring Grandma home to live with them!

Mrs. Stevens reminded Allie about the big extra room near the kitchen. She told Allie that she could help Grandma pick out new paint and curtains, something really special. The room had its own bathroom and two big windows that faced the backyard garden. Allie thought it would be perfect!

Allie learned a lot about Alzheimer's disease during the next few months. Allie and her dad went to the library and looked it up on the computer. She learned that nobody could catch Alzheimer's disease from Grandma or anyone else. She learned that important doctors were studying Alzheimer's disease every day. She learned that doctors were always looking for new medicines to help Grandma and new treatments to make her feel better.

After Grandma came to live with them, Allie learned other things about Alzheimer's disease too. She learned some days were really hard. Some days Grandma got really angry, for no reason at all! She learned that taking care of Grandma and Matthew was a lot of work for her mother. Mrs. Stevens didn't have much free time to spend with Allie anymore.

When Grandma moved in, she loved her new, big room! Allie had helped her pick out her favorite shade of purple paint. It was nice and cheerful! Grandma smiled when Allie and her mom hung white lace curtains above the wide garden windows. Allie's dad moved a lot of Grandma's furniture in and brought over her favorite old rocking chair.

Soon Allie began to understand that Grandma couldn't help the way she acted or felt. It was part of living with Alzheimer's disease. The whole family learned to be very patient. Before long, Allie's dad hired the nurse down the street to stay with Grandma and Matthew every Sunday afternoon. It was good for Allie and her parents to take a break once in a while.

When the afternoon weather was warm and sunny, Allie helped Grandma put on a sweater. They had a new Saturday tradition now, a short walk in the backyard. Afterwards, they each picked wildflowers from the garden. Grandma loved to kneel down and smell the different fragrances. Of course, the purple flowers were her favorite!

Just before Allie's bedtime, she spent some "alone" time with Grandma. Grandma helped pick out a picture book for Allie to read aloud. Together, they snuggled in Grandma's cozy bed.

Allie didn't like this thing called Alzheimer's disease very much. She wished that Grandma didn't have it. Then, cuddled up with Grandma, she remembered what her mother had said from the very beginning. Allie had to think about the "positive" things.

The most important thing Allie learned about Alzheimer's disease was to love her very special grandma ... no matter what!

To order additional copies of Allie Learns About Alzheimer's Disease or inquire about our quantity discounts for schools, hospitals, and affiliated organizations, contact us at 1-800-999-6884.

From our *Special Kids in School*® series

Taking A.D.D. to School
Taking Asthma to School
Taking Autism to School
Taking Cancer to School
Taking Cerebral Palsy to School
Taking Cystic Fibrosis to School
Taking Diabetes to School
Taking Food Allergies to School
Taking Seizure Disorders to School
Taking Tourette Syndrome to School
...and others coming soon!

From our new *Healthy Habits for Kids*™ series

There's a Louse in My House
A Fun Story about Kids and Head Lice
Coming soon ...
Playtime Is Exercise!
A Fun Story about Exercise and Play

And from our *Substance Free Kids*® series

Smoking STINKS!!™
A Heartwarming Story about the
Importance of Avoiding Tobacco

Other books available now!

SPORTSercise!
A School Story about
Exercise-Induced Asthma

ZooAllergy
A Fun Story about Allergy
and Asthma Triggers

Rufus Comes Home
Rufus the Bear with Diabetes™
A Story about Diagnosis and
Acceptance

The ABC's of Asthma
An Asthma Alphabet Book
for Kids of All Ages

Taming the Diabetes Dragon
A Story about Living Better
with Diabetes

Trick-or-Treat for Diabetes
A Halloween Story for Kids
Living with Diabetes

A portion of the proceeds from all our publications is donated to various charities to help fund important medical research and education. We work hard to make a difference in the lives of children with chronic conditions and/or special needs. Thank you for your support.